The Spirit of
THE SOUTH

Text
Bill Harris

Photography
Colour Library Books Ltd
Black Star
Woodfin Camp & Associates

Photo Editor
Annette Lerner

Design
Sally Strugnell

Commissioning
Andrew Preston
Edward Doling
Laura Potts

Editorial
Louise Houghton
Gill Waugh

Production
Ruth Arthur
Sally Connolly
David Proffit
Karen Staff
Andrew Whitelaw

Director of Production
Gerald Hughes

CLB 2660
© 1991 Colour Library Books Ltd, Godalming, Surrey, England.
All rights reserved.
This 1991 edition published by Portland House,
distributed by Outlet Book Company, Inc, a Random House Company,
225 Park Avenue South, New York, New York 10003.
Color separations by Scantrans Pte Ltd, Singapore.
Printed and bound in Singapore.
ISBN 0 517 05308 X
8 7 6 5 4 3 2 1

The Spirit of
THE SOUTH

PORTLAND HOUSE

1   VIRGINIA

2   NORTH CAROLINA

3   SOUTH CAROLINA

4   TENNESSEE

5   LOUISIANA

6   MISSISSIPPI

7   ALABAMA

8   GEORGIA

9   FLORIDA

CONTENTS

The breathtaking spectacle of Hanging Rock in North Carolina.

When the first English-born colonists began moving inland from Tidewater Virginia they had already met native-born Indians, and though the experience had been mixed, they had a good idea of what to expect in terms of human contact. But what some found went far beyond the expectations of any of them.

In a wild valley southwest of Jamestown they were met by blond-haired, blue-eyed people who not only understood English, but some of whom could also read and write. They themselves didn't have any idea why they were more like the newcomers than the savages they lived among, except for a vague legend about what they called white gods who had visited their ancestors. Their descendants, known as Lumbees, still live in the backwoods of North Carolina, and after more than two centuries the mystery of how they got there has still not been solved. One theory is that they are descendants of the survivors of the lost colony of Roanoke that vanished from the face of the earth in 1589. In all the years since then, no one has been able to come up with anything better than vague theories about what became of those colonists, and it never occurred to the migrating Virginians that the Lumbees might be related to those first English settlers in the New World. Although less than twenty years after the Roanoke colonists disappeared, Jamestown's official historian recorded that there was a tribe of Indians to the northwest who lived in two-story stone houses and raised tame turkeys in their yards. He wrote that they had acquired their civilized ways from four men, two boys and a young maid who had survived a massacre at Roanoke. Captain John Smith, the leader of the Jamestown colony, also reported that the survivors themselves were "yet alive, within fifty miles of our fort." But neither he nor the historian offered any proof, and the search for the original settlers of the American South ended there.

Their story began in 1584, when Fort Raleigh was established on Roanoke Island off the coast of present-day North Carolina, not far from the spot where, in 1903, the Wright Brothers proved it was possible for man to fly. It was the first English toehold in America, but its birth was almost accidental.

The Spanish and the French had already made attempts to colonize the continent, but England's Queen Elizabeth was unimpressed. She finally responded to public pressure by sending Sir Humphrey Gilbert to find a likely spot to settle, but Sir Humphrey was unimpressed, too. Fortunately for the future of England in America, he was lost at sea on the way home and was never able to confirm the Queen's suspicions in person. In an attempt to recover her investment, she sent Walter Raleigh, Gilbert's half-brother and a court favorite, to continue the search. His ships took him to Roanoke Island, where he found the natives friendly though poverty stricken. All they were able to give him in exchange for iron hatchets were some deerskins and a bag of dried tobacco leaves. Raleigh didn't need deerskins, and the quality of the tobacco wasn't up to snuff compared to the leaves that were already being exported from the West Indies, so he captured two of the natives and took them back to England with him.

For some reason, that was what it took to convince Queen Elizabeth that this America might be worth something after all, and she came up with the funds to establish an English colony there. At the same time, she named the place Virginia in honor of herself, "the Virgin Queen," and knighted Raleigh to give him more status in the New World. Sir Walter wasted no time, and within a year he dispatched a hundred of his countrymen to Roanoke Island. The colonizers were more interested in finding gold than a new life, but as it turned out they found neither, and when Sir Francis Drake stopped at the island on his way home from plundering Spanish settlements in Central America, they talked him into taking them back with him. Raleigh responded by sending out a second colonizing expedition, but this time he agreed to let the men take their wives along.

Their intention was to settle further north, but the Portuguese captain who had been hired to command their three ships dropped them at Roanoke in spite of their protests, and they faced the same problems as had their predecessors. And before long they also had another little problem. One of the women, Eleanor Dare, gave birth to a daughter, the first English child born in America, and Eleanor named the child Virginia in honor of the new land. Virginia's grandfather, John White, went back to England for fresh supplies a few months after she was born, but before he could return war broke out between England and Spain, and there was no available ship to take him to Virginia for two long years. By then the Roanoke colonists had vanished without trace.

In spite of their ominous end, the new English king, James I, was intrigued by the possibilities of colonizing America and, after ordering Raleigh's execution, started over with a clean slate by granting a charter allowing the newly-formed London Company to settle lands between Spanish Florida and the Chesapeake Bay. It was under that charter that three ships sailed into the Chesapeake in April, 1607. One of the 105 colonists aboard didn't see the spring flowers and the lush countryside as they headed toward the river they would call James in honor of their king. His name was John Smith. He would soon be their leader, even their savior, but in his first moments in the New World, Captain Smith was in irons in the hold of one of the ships.

Before they left England, King James had placed the names of the men he wanted to run the colony in a sealed box and given strict orders that it should not be opened until after they landed in Virginia. Smith was a man born to the job, and it was apparent to most of the would-be Virginians right away. But some of those who fancied themselves a better choice began a whispering campaign, accusing him of plotting to kill them and make himself "King of Virginia." Because of the force of his personality enough of the others believed it, and it was decided to confine him to the brig until James's wishes could be made known.

When the sealed orders were opened, Smith was among those named to the ruling council, and he was freed. His enemies made sure freedom was all he got, and he had no voice in the colony's affairs, but there was another voice heard in the wilderness. It belonged to Powhatan, the absolute ruler of some twenty Indian tribes on the shores of the Chesapeake. He seemed friendly enough, but as time went by it became obvious that he didn't like the English, and that made the Jamestown colonists very nervous, indeed. They had the advantage of guns, but they were hopelessly outnumbered, more than fifty to one, and they turned for help to the only trained soldier among them, Captain Smith. His first act was to replace their little tent city with one made of wood surrounded by a high palisade, and then he began forays into Powhatan's realm to try to head off any hostilities. His trips were generally successful and added to the settlers' knowledge of their surroundings, but every time Smith left Jamestown his enemies there took it as a signal to replace him. And if that wasn't enough, the Indians started to turn against him, too. They got him first.

Smith was taken to Powhatan's court, where he was kept as a showpiece for several months. When he wasn't being paraded in front of visiting tribal chiefs, the king ordered him to entertain his favorite among his thirty children, a twelve-year-old girl named Pocahontas. The Captain had been an armorer in his younger days and spent the time teaching the little girl how to make metal trinkets and beads. In return she taught him her language and learned English, and a great friendship grew between the Indian princess and the soldier of fortune who had become famous in the civilized world fighting Turks for the Archduke of Austria.

Then, suddenly, Powhatan became bored with his prisoner and ordered him brought to trial. It was done with great ceremony at a feast for two hundred of the king's courtiers that was clearly intended to be Smith's last meal. Before it was over, he was forced to place his head on a stone, and the braves lined up with clubs, waiting for a chance to dash his brains out. But before any of them could move in for the kill, Pocahontas pushed him aside and defiantly placed her own head on the stone. Powhatan was impressed and, as Smith later wrote, seemed content that he "should live to make him hatchets and her beads, bells and copper." He also made the soldier his adopted son and offered him a kingdom of his own, but Pocahontas interceded again and convinced her father that Captain Smith should be returned to Jamestown. More than that, she also saved the colony from starvation, making frequent trips through the long winter, bringing gifts of game and other foodstuffs.

Smith's enemies never stopped harassing him, and now they began spreading rumors that he and the princess were contemplating marriage, which would give him the royal status they had been predicting all along. But he confounded them by sailing back to Britain, and Pocahontas surprised them by marrying a different Englishman, John Rolfe, who took her home to England, where she died at the age of twenty-two. But she is recalled to this day in the Tidewater as the savior of Virginia.

Actually, she was only the first of them. The story of the establishment of the Virginia colony is punctuated at every turn with suffering and heroism, and a determination to succeed that eventually spread to all of America, but it is still remembered, almost reverently, as an enduring tradition of the American South. After John Smith left Jamestown, the settlement was plunged into what its historians called "the starving time." In a single winter, the community of five hundred people was reduced to just sixty-five, and when Sir Thomas Gates arrived in the spring with two ships the survivors convinced him that he should take them home to England and burn Jamestown to the ground. History seemed ready to repeat itself with a second lost colony, but as the ships were hoisting their sails fate stepped in. Another ship sailed up the river and its commander, Lord De la Warr, was horrified at the thought that Englishmen, even these emaciated creatures, would give up. He refused to allow them to leave and took control of their destiny. De la Warr was a hard master, even handing out death sentences to men who didn't pull their weight, but in a few years the colony was thriving. By the time the Pilgrims arrived up north at Plymouth Rock, the population of Virginia had already grown to over 2,500, and they had established a representative government that would eventually become the model for the entire United States. Meanwhile, England and the rest of Europe had developed a passion for smoking, despite the fact that King James himself denounced it as a custom "loathsome to the eye, hateful to the nose, harmful to the brain and dangerous to the lungs" and tobacco, in the form of improved strains introduced by John Rolfe, became comparable to the gold the earliest settlers had come to Virginia to find.

By 1640, 14,000 Englishmen had emigrated to Virginia, but the population of the colony had actually grown by less than half that number. Most of those lost died of disease, and many starved to death, but hundreds were victims of an Indian uprising that began after the Emperor Powhatan died and lasted more than two decades. But through it all, none of them considered going back to England. They had become Virginians. Many of them were the younger sons of landed gentry back in England, which made them a breed apart from the typical settlers who headed for the New World in the seventeenth century. Because of their family background, they didn't migrate to America to find a better way of life, but rather to duplicate the life of their older brothers, who were the heirs to the family estates. Most of them were determined to out-do their brothers, in fact, and many succeeded, in spite of the hardships of living on a wild frontier surrounded by savages, and the fiercely competitive spirit of others like them.

After having the territory all to themselves for nearly thirty years they lost a slice of it when King Charles gave a land grant to George Calvert, Lord Baltimore, whose son Cecilius established a colony he called Maryland in 1634. Virginia had been created as a business enterprise for the benefit of London merchants, but Calvert was given a charter along with the grant that allowed him to set up his own ground rules for colonization. Apart from proclaiming that it would be forbidden to discriminate against his fellow Catholics, he envisioned a place where the lords of a few huge manors would control the land and the destiny of the people. As it turned out, the same hard-driving types that had found opportunity in Virginia were attracted to Maryland, too, and the manor system that was intended to give power to a chosen few never had a chance. The men who became powerful were the ones who worked at it, just as had been the case in the older colony. But in the process Catholics got short shrift. Most of Maryland's population was Protestant, and though they followed Lord Baltimore's wishes in tolerating Catholics in their midst, they managed to turn Maryland into a royal colony by 1691 and made the Church of England its official religion. At the same time they denied Catholics the right to vote or hold office, or to hold religious services anywhere but in the privacy of their own homes. The proprietorship was restored to the Calvert family in 1715, but the fourth Lord Baltimore had by that time become a Protestant himself, and he paid little attention to his grandfather's original plan, although he did make life easier for Catholics in Maryland. Nor did he make any attempt to implement the original idea of a feudal society. It was probably too late. There were more than 65,000 people in the colony by then, and most of them seemed to like the proposition that all of them were in control of their own destiny.

But old ideas die hard. Civil war in England had overthrown the monarchy, but when it was restored the new king, Charles II, rewarded eight of his supporters with a land grant south of Virginia. In gratitude, they named it Carolina, after the Latin version of their benefactor's name. They envisioned a feudal colony that made Lord Baltimore's ideas seem almost egalitarian, but like him they were really more interested in turning a profit. In their eagerness they began a promotion campaign to lure settlers who could make the land productive, and it proved most effective among Englishmen who had originally migrated to the island of Barbados, but who had arrived there too late to acquire enough land for the big plantations of their dreams. Because they were driven by a dream, and were already one step removed from British ideas, they had no use for a society that included a nobility. But if there is nobility in hard work, there was plenty of that facing the new Carolinians. There was land enough to match their grand plans, but making it productive was another matter. They realized from the beginning that their best hope was in cultivating rice, but the colony was well into its thirtieth year before they were able to find strains that could make it profitable, and it took twenty more years to find the best way to harvest and thresh it. But once they solved the problem the colony prospered and the population, which hadn't topped a thousand in almost fifty years, began growing at the rate of another thousand a year.

King Charles's original land grant included, among other territory, all of what is now North and South Carolina, and although the proprietors didn't have that distinction in mind, it was obvious from the start that there would be one. They established their main settlement at Charleston, but in a few years Virginians began moving south to the Outer Banks and then started establishing inland settlements. By the turn of the century there were ten times as many people living in the northern colony, known as Albemarle, as there were in Charleston, and though they were subject to the rule of the Carolina proprietors their destiny was different, and in 1719 the charter was altered to create North Carolina as a separate royal colony. In its southern reaches planters grew rice, like the South Carolinians, and further north they followed the lead of the Virginians by growing tobacco. But, in between, the colony thrived through the production of turpentine and other products of the thick pine forests they found when they pushed into the interior.

The Southern colonies were all prosperous and growing fast by the end of the first quarter of the eighteenth century, but there was a fly in the ointment: the Spanish still controlled Florida. The English knew that unless they were able to secure the rest of the South by populating it, there was nothing to stop the Spanish from moving northward. They solved the problem with an experiment. In 1732 a board of trustees was formed and given a twenty-one-year lease on a stretch of territory in the southern reaches of the Carolina grant, a place they called Georgia. The trustees were English philanthropists, who envisioned a colony that would be a haven for imprisoned debtors and others who needed a second chance in their lives. The first of them arrived in the company of James Oglethorpe, one of the trustees, and established a settlement at Savannah. The philanthropists were generous, paying for the passage of the new Georgians and helping them get established once they arrived. But there was a price tag. No one was allowed to expand his holding beyond five hundred acres and no one was allowed to own slaves. They were also told not to compete with their neighbors by growing rice or tobacco, and encouraged instead to produce such things as silk, wine and spices, things that were in demand in England but not available through any of the crown's other colonies. But, like their neighbors in the Carolinas, Virginia and Maryland, the settlers had minds of their own and they were determined to become successful in their own way. It was a happy day for them when the trustee's lease expired in 1752 and they were free to get on with their dreams. It was an infectious feeling. In the next twenty years their numbers grew from 5,000 to 25,000.

It had been more than a century and a half since the first Englishmen had set down roots in the American South, and they had been joined by Germans, French and others to create an identity a little bit different from that in the colonies north of the Chesapeake. The roots of the entire southern experience had been firmly planted in Virginia, and if the Virginians created the spirit of the South, they were more than ready to make a contribution to the spirit of America itself.

For all their drive and resilience, and their qualities of rugged individualism, colonial Southerners, especially the Virginians, were staunchly loyal to the English king. During the years when the monarchy was dissolved, some of the Cavaliers who had fought against Oliver Cromwell in the English Civil War found a haven and a warm welcome in the Southern colonies. It was the first glimmering of a difference between North and South in America, because Cromwell was a Puritan and had the enthusiastic support of his coreligionists in New England. In Virginia, on the other hand, the Assembly proclaimed Charles II King of England as soon as the news reached them that his father had been beheaded. As far as they were concerned the monarchy still existed, even though the Roundheads had taken control and

A mother and son searching for sea shells on the Atlantic Coast at Savannah, Georgia.

stayed in power on the other side of the Atlantic for eleven years.

Among the Royalists who arrived during those years were families with names that included those of Mason and Lee, Carter and Randolph, whose descendants changed the course of American history. But at the same time, there were other new arrivals whose names may not have seemed important, but who changed the character of the South. Trouble in France brought French Huguenots, who also found a haven in the Carolinas. Both Scotland and Ireland found Virginia a convenient place to get rid of political activists, and their countrymen followed them to America in huge numbers. And not all the migration to the South came from across the ocean. English Quakers moved southward from Pennsylvania, and Welsh settlers moved down the Chesapeake, too, bringing their Baptist religion to unnerve the Anglicans who controlled the Southern colonies through their church. German immigrants who had arrived in America through Northern ports began establishing farms in the Piedmont, and New Englanders transplanted themselves into the South, adding their own values to the mix. Slowly, the character of the Southern colonies changed, from a bit of Britain in the wilderness to a society unique, not only to the British Empire, but to the New World.

But not all of the South answered to the King of England. French explorers had made the Mississippi River their king's turf in the early sixteenth century, and even now the state they named Lousiana in his honor has a French accent. It wasn't until 1803 that President Thomas Jefferson negotiated with Napoleon to make it part of the United States, but though he was a Southerner himself, he was much more interested in the territory to the north and west that was part of the deal. Another nine years went by before Congress thought of buying the so-called Florida Parishes, north of the Mississippi Delta and east of the river itself, and adding them to a newly-created state. But the area had been settled a hundred years earlier, and the majority of the people who called it home didn't speak English and didn't care to learn it. Another hundred years passed before the state legislature got around to conducting its business in just one language, but even though that language was English, the laws they administered were based on time-honored French codes.

The French had established themselves along the Gulf Coast, too, and almost twenty years before they began building New Orleans they had a colony at Biloxi, Mississippi, and were protecting their interests against the Spanish from Fort Conde, which eventually became Mobile, Alabama. The fort was, in fact, the capital of the French empire until 1722, when their government moved to New Orleans. But if the Spanish kept them on their toes, French colonists east of the Mississippi River had their hands full dealing with Indian tribes who thought they were the ones who owned the place. The Spanish tried to disabuse them of the notion when Hernando de Soto took on the Choctaw in 1540 and wiped out thousands of braves in one of the bloodiest battles ever fought in North America. But he left the survivors with a resolve to resist that slowed growth in the Deep South for nearly two hundred years.

In the end the Indians provided another wedge between the interests of North and South. Except for the single term of John Adams, Southerners had controlled the presidency of the United States for all of the first thirty-five years of the republic. When Massachusetts-born John Quincy Adams was elected, he planned an administration that would be more national in character than those of his predecessors, but even after more than a quarter century of independence most Americans were far more loyal to their native states than to the idea of a United States.

The Federal Government had made a treaty with the Cherokees giving them the right to their ancestral lands in Northwestern Georgia. But the Georgians themselves had other ideas. Adams objected when they began surveying the Cherokee land to divide it up for settlement, but Congress carried the day and the Indians lost in the name of state's rights. It was one of the issues that carried Tennessean Andrew Jackson into the White House. He was well known as an Indian fighter, but he shared the view of most Southerners that Indians were like little children, and that it was the responsibility of the white man to care for them rather than kill them. He also believed, as did most of his neighbors, that the red men could never be happy in a civilized environment but that, on the other hand, the whites could never be comfortable with savages in their midst, no matter how childlike they may be. The solution, he announced in his first State of the Union address, was to accept the inevitable fact that Georgians and Cherokees were like oil and water, and that if the Indians were not moved west across the Mississippi, states like Georgia and the Carolinas would eventually be torn apart. Since it was believed that Washington's responsibility was to protect the rights of the individual states, it followed in Jackson's mind that the original residents should be evicted under Federal pressure. It took until Jackson's second term to make the Cherokees understand, and even then he had to sweeten the deal by paying them $5 million for their ancestral lands and giving them new lands in what is now Oklahoma. In spite of Jackson's generosity they still had to be forced to go, and about a thousand of them headed for the hills of North Carolina, where their descendants still live. Learning from his experience, Jackson drove a harder bargain with the Choctaws and Chickasaws further south. He gave them free prairie land in exchange for the woods and swamps of their homeland, but told them that if they didn't go every man, woman and child would be killed. They accepted his offer, and Georgia, Alabama and Mississippi were safe at last for white settlement.

But in the same year the Indians headed west, the South heard a new challenge to its way of life coming from the North. Up in Boston an activist named William Lloyd Garrison began publishing a newspaper he called *The Liberator* to spread his idea that all slaves should be set free immediately, and that their owners, whom Garrison painted as immoral, should not be compensated. When he began his career as a publisher in 1831, most Americans, both Northerners and Southerners, dismissed Garrison as a wild-eyed radical. But when his followers began mailing anti-slavery broadsides into the Southern states, President Jackson responded with an executive order that no publication of any kind could be delivered unless the addressee had requested it. He also ruled that petitions to Congress could not become the subject of any debate. But the subject of slavery had been part of the national debate from the earliest colonial times.

Clearing the wilderness and creating productive farms was a challenge everyone shared, and the only way it could be met was with a large workforce. Most of those who came from Europe were willing to work, but the amount of work required just to feed a family was overwhelming, and it was clear that if a man was to have any luxury at all it was necessary to have other men working for him. The Southern colonies felt the problem most strongly because, although the climate was harsh in New England, that of the South brought discomfort and disease, and most prospective settlers who could afford to pay their own way to the New World chose to go to ports north of Philadelphia.

Southern businessmen and planters evened the odds by taking advantage of a British law that allowed men who could afford it to buy servants, who would work without pay for the duration of a contract. The Americans had the advantage of an almost unlimited labor pool, both in England and in other parts of Europe, made up of people more than willing to sign such contracts in return for their passage to the New World and a new life. It was estimated that as many as three-quarters of the settlers who arrived in the seventeeth-century South had signed such agreements, and that when their contracts expired, most went to work for wages and invested their earnings in land, which in turn made it necessary for them to begin importing indentured servants of their own.

The contracts typically lasted five or six years, and when a servant was freed an expensive replacement usually needed to be found. In an attempt to cut their losses, some planters traded with friendly Indians for captives from other tribes to use as slaves. But, since the Indian slaves knew the territory better than their English masters, it was easy for them to vanish into the woods. On the other hand, a way out of the dilemma had been in their midst since 1619, when about twenty blacks arrived in Virginia, one year before the Pilgrims landed at Plymouth, seven years before the Dutch bought Manhattan Island, and fifteen years before Lord Baltimore began planning the Maryland colony.

Another half century passed before selling blacks for life took hold in the American colonies, and even then the African population of Virginia was well under 500. The price of a black slave was usually double that of a white servant, but for a man of means it was a way of flaunting his affluence, and in the long run the lifetime term made owning blacks a better economic proposition than replacing indentured servants every half dozen years. By 1700 all

Timson House, at the corner of Prince George and Nassau streets, Colonial Williamsburg.

the Southern colonies had substantial African populations and were firmly committed to slavery. This was so even in Georgia, where the institution had been expressly forbidden during its first twenty-one years. The idea was neither new nor unique. Blacks were being captured in Africa and sold in Spain long before Columbus discovered America. And there wasn't a Colonial power in Europe that didn't engage in the trade. It has been estimated that as many as ten million people were forcibly exported from Africa to the Americas, but less than half a million of them were shipped to the United States. In the opinion of some, they were the lucky ones. When slave trading was outlawed in the United States in 1808, the country's black population had reached a million, and by the outbreak of the Civil War there were more than four million. While slaves were dying in other places, they were thriving and raising families in the American South.

Slavery allowed the owners of large tracts of land to turn them into successful plantations producing tobacco or rice, indigo or sugar cane. Their markets were strong and their profits were limited only by their production, which the blacks they owned helped them increase dramatically. And when cotton became king in the early-nineteenth century, after the Indians had been removed from the deep South, it was the availability of slaves that made it possible. Most planters regarded their slaves as an investment in their business, and they knew that working them to death, as often happened in the Caribbean islands, didn't make good business sense.

The big planters loom large in the history of the South, but the overwhelming majority of their neighbors are more properly called farmers. Through the middle of the nineteenth century, and even well into this present one, the number of Southerners living in cities and towns was insignificant compared to the rural population. Most of them worked their own land, but they ranked rather lower on the social scale than the plantation owners who are more closely related to the corporate farmers of today. They dreamed of the day when their hard work would allow them to expand their holdings and make them members of the elite, but in the meantime they had the right to vote and they had the pride of being in control of their own destiny. Beneath them were the poor whites, often landless or unskilled, who barely eked out a living.

But even the poorest of them took pride in the fact that there was a class even lower than themselves: the blacks. Even though some of them were descendants of indentured servants and had never been a part of the slave system, and others had long since been freed and were contributing members of society, their black skin set them apart and kept them, as the whites often said, "in their place." It was a concept deeply rooted in the European psyche that for centuries had been reducing the world to black and white, the former usually symbolizing darkness and evil. Explorers who had visited Africa used the metaphor in their descriptions of the people they found there as a subhuman species whom God had surely colored black as a symbol of their inferiority. It helped them justify the practice of capturing those people and selling them into slavery, and it also helped slave owners square the idea with their consciences. Because, above all else, a love of liberty runs deep in the Southern psyche.

Virginian Patrick Henry, whose challenge, "give me liberty or give me death" helped unite all the colonies in 1775, was a slave owner. But, in the same speech, he also said to those who were opposed to going to war against England: "Is life so dear, or peace so sweet, as to be purchased at the price of chains and slavery?" Thomas Jefferson, who wrote that all men are endowed by their creator with inalienable rights that include liberty, was also a slave owner. So was George Washington and, in fact, so were nearly all the Southern leaders who lent their impressive stature to the cause that made liberty the cornerstone of the American experience. To be sure, most of them denounced the institution. Jefferson noted that most of his fellow Southerners were " ... zealous for their own liberties, but trampling on those of others." Washington cautioned that unless Americans united against England, they would all become slaves " ... as the blacks we rule over with such arbitrary sway." But Patrick Henry probably summed up the mood of all of them when he said of his own slaves: " ... I am drawn along by the general inconvenience of living without them. I will not, I cannot justify it."

But in spite of their eloquence, the institution of slavery survived the war for independence. In some ways, in fact, the soul searching of the 1770s bound the South more tightly together. And if the war united the American states, it was clearer than ever that their interests were divided, and that the line between them was at the northern end of the Chesapeake, the same line that had been drawn by King James when he chartered the London Company to settle the territory between Florida and the bay back in 1606.

But the King hadn't given much thought to eventual westward expansion, and even the well-known Mason-Dixon Line, which established the southern boundary of Pennsylvania and became the symbolic dividing line between North and South, didn't extend west of the Alleghenies. When Americans began crossing the mountains and the Louisiana Purchase opened the West, Northern politicians began questioning whether the new territories should allow slavery. The Constitution had left the issue up to the individual states, and to secure support for ratification in the South, the framers had agreed that representation in Congress based on population would take slaves into account. They didn't count as equals, but every black slave was recognized as three-fifths of a citizen, and as far as the Northern states were concerned the numbers tipped the balance of power against them. The South, on the other hand, looked northward and saw a growing population and a thriving economy draining its own power on the national scene. The balance was clearly shaky, but when Florida and Texas were admitted to the Union in 1845 the score was even, with fifteen states allowing slavery and fifteen forbidding it. For many Southerners, though, the end of the road was in sight. A fight was looming over the still undeveloped West, and Congress was already debating whether slavery should be outlawed in the half-million square miles of territory won in the Mexican War.

After their hero Andrew Jackson had disappointed them by putting forward Martin Van Buren, a Northerner, as his successor, Southern leaders formed a new political grouping they called the Whig party, from a British political movement opposed to the power of the king. Their first successful presidential candidate, Zachary Taylor, was as true a son of the South as a man could be. Born in Virginia and raised on the Kentucky frontier, he lived in Louisiana, and he owned a cotton plantation in Mississippi tended by one hundred slaves. He had distinguished himself as a Major General in the Mexican War, which made him an attractive candidate in the North as well, but in the deep South folks were sure that they had him in their hip pocket. They were wrong as it turned out. One of his first acts was to push for statehood for California and New Mexico, neither of which had yet been settled by slaveholders, and which would surely be counted among the free states unless time was allowed for more Southerners to move in. The Southern Whigs did what they could to get the President to change his mind, but he had another trait they all cherished – stubbornness – and he refused to be moved. They themselves were moved to hold a meeting to consider the possibility of removing themselves from the Union. The tension ended when the President suddenly died, and Congress managed to approve a compromise that admitted California as a free state, but left the territories of Utah and New Mexico open to a future vote. It ended talk of secession, but it also marked the beginning of the end for the Whigs.

Six years later, a new political party fielded a candidate in the presidential election of 1856 and, although he lost, it was clear that these people who called themselves Republicans intended to stay on the national scene for a long time to come. There were almost no Southerners among them, and almost no Southerners would have dreamed of voting for a party whose platform made no bones about calling slavery barbaric and whose candidates routinely demonstrated "hostility to the domestic institutions of the Southern States." The Democrats considered themselves the great protectors of those Southern institutions, but by the election of 1860 they were divided among themselves, the Southern wing of the party nominating its own candidates, and die-hard Whigs forming a third party called the Constitutional Union, which claimed to hold the key to Southern salvation. When the ballots were counted, the three candidates shared sixty percent of the popular vote, but the winner in the electoral college was Republican Abraham Lincoln.

It was the first time in the history of the country that Southerners were without a voice in national affairs and, to make matters worse, the voices they heard in Washington were predicting that the Republicans were committed to restoring "justice" to the government.

Whatever the word may have meant up North, in the South it was a clear signal that they were about to lose their slaves and become enslaved to a government that had no reason to listen to them. They themselves had abandoned the Democrats. Nearly half of them had voted with the new, third party, which faded out of existence after the election. They felt as though they had been left out on their own, and between Lincoln's election and his inauguration, seven of the fifteen Southern States removed themselves from the Union and formed a new nation, the Confederate States of America. Within two months of the rebels attacking Fort Sumter in Charleston Harbor, and Federal troops opposing them, the four states of the Upper South joined the Confederacy. The so-called Border States: Missouri, Maryland, Delaware and Kentucky, stayed with the Union, as did the western half of Virginia, which in effect seceded from the State rather than the Union.

The war lasted three days short of four years. In that time the South lost well over a half million men, nearly ten percent of its white male population, and as many more carried the scars of their wounds for the rest of their lives. Almost all of the railroads were gone, few factories were left and there was hardly a farm or plantation that hadn't become a wasteland. In terms of dollars, the cost was close to $7 billion. But all that was only the first cost.

Even the large number of Southerners who had been opposed to the institution of slavery were willing to defend the right of their neighbors to own slaves, because they believed that a government that could take away that right was capable of enslaving all of its citizens. The historical effect of the Civil War was freedom for black slaves, but it was a rare white Southerner in the second half of the 19th century who didn't believe that the yoke had been shifted to their shoulders.

The Civil War also increased the power of the Federal Government over the individual states by demonstrating that it was foolhardy, even suicidal, for them to try to stand outside the system. But more important to Southerners, who had always been passionate on the subject of states' rights, it had made the differences between North and South more apparent to more American families than ever before. Even people who never read a newspaper, never voted in an election, and never noticed that there were other people living more than a few miles from their own front door had been touched by the war, and "us" versus "them" became a part of the fabric of American life on both sides of the Mason-Dixon Line well into the 20th century.

In our own generation, there is still a vague feeling in most parts of America that the South is a little bit different from the rest of the country, and the rugged individualism that goes back to colonial times makes Southerners perfectly happy to let many of the stereotypes stand. But if you scratch beneath the surface, you'll probably find that they are as much a part of mainstream America as if they hailed from the traditionally industrial north.

On the other hand, that word "tradition" still makes all the difference. Even though the South seems to be catching up with the industrial side of America, as recently as a generation ago the Southern States were still largely filled with small farms and small towns, where survival often depended on self-sufficiency. A man was expected to take care of himself and his family, and the experience of history had taught him to be cautious of strangers, no matter how well-meaning they might seem to be. It gave strangers a strange view of Southerners that still persists, even though, contrary to the belief of some, it is as unlikely that anyone will be challenged to a duel on the streets of Bridgeport, Alabama, as in Bridgeport, Connecticut. That isn't to say that a dispute in the South might have been settled with pistols at fifty paces as recently as fifty years ago, or that no one there cares about personal honor any longer. Times have changed and so has the South, but a typical Southern man in the 1990s, even though he may wear a three-piece suit and work in an airconditioned office, is closer than most Americans in spirit to the frontiersmen of the 1790s, who respected nature but never stopped fighting it.

It is rare for a man with roots in the South not to have roots in the land as well. If he himself wasn't raised on a farm, his father probably was, or at least he had close friends or relatives who were. It was only natural that such a person would find fun in the outdoors. A Southern boy who had never treed a possum, nor watched the sun come up over a pond that everyone swore was the home of the granddaddy of all the bass in creation, was considered underprivileged. He might have just dreamed about bear hunting, but it's a good bet he had won a footrace, or at least tried to, and spent some of his time on a fence rail admiring fast horses. One of his cherished rights of passage might have been feeling the white heat of raw whiskey in his throat and clearing it with a blood-curdling rebel yell. And if the child is indeed father to the man, many of those boyhood moments went into the creation of the "good ole' boy" many outsiders believe is the typical Southern man. Some of them believe it themselves, even though in the South, as everywhere else in America, the opportunities for fun in the great unspoiled outdoors are vanishing. Swamps and ponds have been drained and forests cleared, small towns have become cities complete with their own sprawling suburbs, and cities have become industrial centers. But many men still carry hunting rifles in their pickup trucks and tow bass boats behind them, because, as everyone knows, you may take the boy out of the country, but you can never take the country out of the boy.

It is a little sad to accept that the average Southerner's way of life is changing, but after more than thirty years of sociological pronouncements that we were all witnessing the birth of the "New South," the Southeastern corner of the United States is giving up some of its individuality and becoming as homogenized as the rest of the country. Whether that is a good thing or not overall remains to be seen. But for now, statistically at least, it is good for the South.

In a time within the memories of most Southerners the races were segregated by both law and custom, and opportunities for both blacks and whites in many Southern States were at the bottom of every scale that was measured, from the quality of education, to health care, to family income. But all that has been swept away. Among other changes, the tide of blacks that had been moving away from the South since the 1930s has been completely reversed. More blacks are going home to the South these days than are leaving it. And, just as significantly, the tourist bureaus in the Southern States are encouraging blacks to sample their famous hospitality at vacation time.

In Alabama, the Bureau of Tourism has distributed nearly a quarter million copies of a special thirty-page brochure that lists attractions of special interest to African-Americans, ranging from a quilting bee organized by black women to a state park near Mobile called "AfricaTown U.S.A." In Mississippi, where the state's director or tourism is a black man, as well as in Georgia and South Carolina, sites important to the Civil Rights movement are proudly maintained by the state governments. And local communities are supporting such landmarks as the Dexter Avenue Memorial Baptist Church in Montgomery, Alabama, where the Rev. Dr. Martin Luther King, Jr. helped organize the city's bus boycott. A museum at Alabama's Tuskegee Institute, honoring the work of George Washington Carver and Booker T. Washington, clocked 275,724 visitors in 1989, up from 60,000 five years earlier. History isn't all that attracts African-American visitors, whose fathers couldn't stay in local hotels or eat in local restaurants, but who represent an estimated $15 billion a year to the South's tourist industry today. Many return for family reunions, bent on impressing the folks back home with how well they've done since leaving, but most are pleasantly surprised to see how well the families they left behind are doing themselves.

The South of the recent past was different from other regions of the country because it hadn't been affected by the waves of European immigrants who arrived in America during the 19th century. Most new arrivals migrated there as native-born Americans from Northern States, and, as heirs to a rural tradition, most tended to stay put once they arrived. The result was that in the last century most of the South's population increase came from the growth of families, rather than from the infusion of new blood. But now its cities are growing faster than the national average, as newcomers arrive from the North and from the Caribbean islands, and local moving companies are busier than ever because native-born Southerners have acquired a wanderlust, not to move out of the region but to relocate within it.

Almost from the time that Americans began aligning themselves within political parties, the so-called Solid South could always be counted on to vote for Democrats and always for white candidates. But the Republicans are doing very nicely in the South these days, and there are more black elected officials in state and local governments there than in any other part of the country. And, significantly, black candidates usually capture higher margins in the South than in the North.

For years sociologists explained the Southern character as being a direct result of the outcome of the Civil War. But now they are saying that Vietnam changed all that, and if they were right in the first place, they are probably right now. There are still plenty of Confederate flags flying in the South, but the symbolism isn't the same as it was a generation ago. There is no doubt that the Southern character is changing and the quality of life is improving. Income is up, and though it is still a bit below the national average, a family in the South can expect a higher take-home pay than a family in the Rocky Mountain States. As far as the Civil War is concerned, the youngsters who will become the next generation of adults are as indifferent to history as are kids in every other part of the country. And even if the war shows up in cartoon form on Saturday morning television, it doesn't seem likely they'll be inspired to fight it all over again.

But if Southerners these days are more inclined to let the dead past bury its dead, their traditions are very much alive, and will probably stay that way for a long time to come. Because, as the song says, good times are not forgotten 'way down south in Dixie.

But there are bad times still remembered there, too. The Civil War left the South devastated, but Reconstruction left it demoralized. Almost immediately after the war ended the United States had a new President, Tennessean Andrew Johnson. His predecessor, Abraham Lincoln, had devised a plan to bring the Confederate States back into the Union, and had put it into effect in the midst of the war in both Louisiana and Arkansas. Elections were held and Lincoln kept his promise to recognize the new State Governments. But Congress refused to admit their Representatives and Senators, and ignored their electoral votes in the 1864 presidential election. The problem, in the eyes of Congress, was that neither state had given the right to vote to blacks, and they corrected the oversight by passing a bill requiring black suffrage. Lincoln vetoed the law and, up to the time of his assassination, neither he nor Congress had come to terms with what should be done to heal the wounds of the war.

Johnson moved quickly, and a few weeks after becoming president he issued a proclamation of amnesty and appointed provisional governors for each of the former Confederate States, with a mandate to hold conventions to draft new constitutions and then to hold free elections. As it happened, Congress was in recess at the time, and by the time they reconvened, all the Southern States except Texas, which hadn't yet had an opportunity to call its election, had voted to rejoin the Union, and had been warmly welcomed back by Andrew Johnson. Under his plan, as had been the case with Lincoln's scheme, Southerners were given back all the property they had lost except for their slaves, and most, except for Confederate leaders and high-ranking officers, were given a general amnesty in return for loyalty to the Union and repudiation of secession.

It was a good beginning, but only a beginning. Though they voted to repudiate secession, most Southerners still believed in their hearts that they had been right in rebelling. Most also looked around them, and the devastation they saw was a constant reminder of the sufferings of the war. And they were gripped with fear about how the freed blacks, a majority of the population in most places, would react to life among their former masters. They responded to the perceived threat with restrictive laws, and before long it was apparent, in the minds of Northern Congressmen at least, that loyalty oaths notwithstanding, not much had really changed in the South.

Congress didn't waste any time reacting, and passed laws that replaced Johnson's governors with military authorities and, in the unkindest cut of all for the South, passed the Fourteenth Amendment to the Constitution, granting civil rights to all citizens, and the Fifteenth, giving equal voting rights to all, regardless of race or color. It marked the beginning of a period still called, even in the South of today, the "Tragic Time." The era historians prefer to call "Reconstruction" is often characterized by tales of blatant corruption by native-born politicians; by stories of manipulation of inexperienced blacks by so-called scalawags and carpetbaggers, who descended on the South from other states to influence elections and raid the public treasuries; and by horror stories of life under the yoke of hated Yankee soldiers, who had been barbaric during the war and only became worse in its aftermath. Some of the stories were true, but modern historians are finding evidence that much of what was being reported at the time was little more than exaggeration and propaganda, in a political war that was raging for political control, to justify the subordination of blacks and to excuse the violence that often went with it.

In fact, the worst aspects of the Tragic Time were caused by the war itself, and the triumph over those hardships would have provided a dramatic source of pride had it not been for the sideshows that were competing with it for attention. More than half the railroads in the Southern States had been destroyed, but with help from the Union Army and from the political and business establishment in the South itself, the tracks and rolling stock were not only replaced, but in less than twenty years the original mileage had more than doubled. It gave Southern farmers easier access to their markets, and made it possible for merchants to offer their customers goods that were considered luxuries before the war. Most important, the steel rails made it possible to begin thinking for the first time about industrialization. Cotton was still king, but after generations of shipping it in raw form, Southerners began building their own textile mills. Union Army men had developed a taste for North Carolina tobacco during the war years, and cigar factories built on the demand. In the 1880s, the Duke brothers perfected a machine that made cigarette manufacturing practical, and within a decade built a corporation that turn-of-the-century trust busters ranked alongside Standard Oil itself as a business too big even for America.

In the years since World War II the Old South has receded even further into the background. When the war started, about forty percent of all Southerners worked on farms, as had their grandfathers. Less than three percent are tied to the land today, and where cotton once grew the fields are more likely to be supporting soybeans, or they may have been replaced by pine forests to support an industry that provides two-thirds of the pulpwood and a quarter of the timber harvested in the entire country. There are almost no family farms left, and very few sharecroppers, and a mule is more likely to represent a photo opportunity than be the keystone of a family's existence. Most of the displaced rural population has found a new home in the cities, which has had an effect on the relaxed outlook that has always made life in the South enviable. Southerners have added traffic jams and pollution, inner city slums and suburban sprawl to their lives, but they are still not ready to give up that elusive quality that has marked the spirit of the South since colonial times.

The novelist James Dickey explained it when he pointed out that, " ... because they feel the South has preserved individuality of region as well as person and has not been homogenized to quite the extent of the rest of the nation. People want those differences."

There is, indeed, a New South. But it still has enough traces of the old to make it different from other parts of America that are all too often interchangeable with each other. The new generations travel more than their parents ever did, and are more likely to be college educated. But the time they've spent away from the traditions they grew up with hasn't changed them, any more than it has changed the country music writer whose main theme is lamenting that his true love has been stolen away, and swearing that he will find a way to win her back.

In spite of its history, some observers are convinced that the South may hold the key to bringing optimism back to America. Because no matter what they've endured, Southerners have always fervently believed that there were better days ahead, and with the emergence of the New South they are beginning to see their faith pay off.

There is new pride in the South. More than forty years ago Hodding Carter, the Pulitzer Prize-winning editor of the *Delta Democrat Times* of Greenville, Mississippi, wrote: " ... No other region has as generous a combination of equitable climate, productive soil in spite of abuse, actual and potential hydroelectric power, timber and mineral reserves and human resources. No other region has made as little productive use of what it embraces.

" ... The sense of immediate identification with a region fortifies the will to make it more nearly perfect and secure; and as the part is strengthened, so is the whole. It is only when loyalty makes the regional patriot blind to imperfection and resentful of inspection that it becomes a destructive force. The obligation to examine, to protest and to propose change must accompany affection."

It took a long time, but the message is finally getting through. Call it the Spirit of the South.

Finite land and infinite sky, Florida style.

VIRGINIA

Shenandoah Farm in Harpers Ferry, one of the most beautiful rural areas in West Virginia.

The Virginia Museum of
Fine Arts in Richmond
offers all kinds of artwork.

Below: cattle muddle in the
mud at a traditional farm
near Rose Hill.

A peaceful site for a hive of activity, a farm at Ground Hog Mountain.

Mabry Mill, a reminder of olden days in the Blue Ridge Parkway.

Military displays using period firearms provide a lively spectacle in Colonial Williamsburg.

Traditional music played in traditional dress and brass-buckled shoes, Williamsburg.

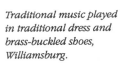

Costumed staff add to the convincing authenticity of recreated Williamsburg in Virginia.

The "Sign of the Rhinoceros" apothecary shop is an unexpected sight in Williamsburg.

John Blair Kitchen is set in delightful gardens off Duke of Gloucester Street in Williamsburg.

Mr and Mrs Fred Fischer personify Southern elegance in the dining room of Westover Plantation.

The balcony in the entrance hall of Jefferson's Monticello joins the north and south wings.

Jefferson's Monticello, one of the nation's most important and beautiful buildings.

Thomas Jefferson, third President of the United States and architect of Monticello in Charlottesville.

Burnt and bleached by the sun on Virginia Beach, coast guards enjoy a chat over a cool drink.

A little girl hugs her pet goat on an impulse inspired by springtime in Virginia.

A family and their mule returning home through the fields with a hot day's tobacco pickings.

The Stone Bridge over Bull Run Creek in Manassas, the site of two Civil War battles.

Perhaps this lady on a "Pick Your Own" strawberry farm believes that forbidden fruit tastes sweeter.

This winter lamb will soon be leaving the security of the lambing shed to take his chances in the snow.

*"As idle as a painted ship
Upon a painted ocean."
Coleridge.*

*The back porch of
Sherwood Forest, home of
President John Tyler in
Charles City County.*

The Tomb of the Unknown Soldier before Arlington House, or Robert E. Lee Memorial.

Blondes pass the time of day with sunburnt brunettes as the evening breeze comes in from the sea at Virginia Beach.

The Iwo Jima Memorial, representing the U.S. Marine Corps' capture of that Pacific Island in 1945.

Great Falls Park on the Potomac River contains the ruins of an eighteenth-century canal and offers splendid scenery.

Celebrations down on the waterfront at Hampton Roads, where James River meets Chesapeake Bay.

Itself like a great bird coming in to land, Dulles International airport is the arrival point for air travellers to Virginia.

James Monroe, graduate of the College of William and Mary, governor of Virginia and fifth President of the United States.

Virginia's State Flower is the dogwood, but azaleas also flourish in the soil of the tenth of the thirteen original states.

Sashes, shutters and a big smile over an overflowing window box make a pretty picture in Norfolk, Virginia.

A costumed blacksmith and wheelwright at Colonial Williamsburg. His apron will have been made by the town saddler.

More uniforms at Bull Run in Manassas National Battlefield, where "Stonewall" Jackson got his nickname.

Restored buildings on Duke of Gloucester Street in Colonial Williamsburg, including the cobbler's and Greenhow Store.

The battlefield upon which Lord Cornwallis surrendered his troops in 1781, thereby assuring the independence of America.

Costumed as Confederate soldiers, staff at the Petersburg National Battlefield prepare to load and fire a cannon.

Pristine soldiers lined up before the equally pristine building of the Virginia Military Institute in Lexington.

Facing page: when the shadows grow long on a fall evening it's good to walk the dog and catch up on local news.

Toes in the sand or toes in the water, Virginia Beach is the place to photograph and be photographed.

Mount Vernon, south of Alexandria, the fascinating home of George Washington from 1754 until his death in 1799.

Fresh, local produce: succulent squash, tasty tomatoes and zesty zucchini.

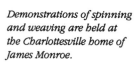

Demonstrations of spinning and weaving are held at the Charlottesville home of James Monroe.

*A pause for a chat with a
neighbor is welcome during
the season-long fall chore
of leaf sweeping.*

Seemingly unaware of the spectacle he makes, this musician is being equally ignored by the assembled company.

Arlington National Cemetry on the banks of the Potomac River contains the graves of thousands who have died for their country.

Sturdy wooden boats with their strong, bleached white sails brilliant against the Virginia sky at Chesapeake Bay.

A bright white sun gilds the Elizabeth River to beaten metal at the end of another perfect day in Virginia.

TENNESSEE

The Great Smoky Mountains, part of the Appalachian Chain which runs through Tennessee and North Carolina.

Musket fire echoes the course of history at Fort Donelson National Military Park, the site of an 1862 Confederate surrender.

The State Capitol in Nashville, Tennessee, an impressive Greek Revival style building completed in 1859.

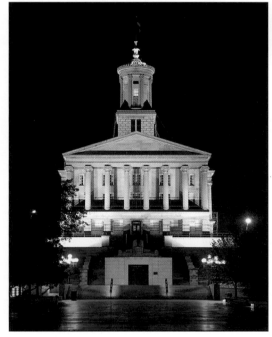

Shining with the sweat of a good day's work, this train driver lives the life that little boys' dreams are made of.

The tomb of Andrew Jackson, seventh President of the United States, in the grounds of his home, The Hermitage.

The crowd rise to their feet in excitement during a match at the University of Tennessee in Knoxville.

Pickwick Landing, a State Resort Park that offers excellent fishing and an eighteen-hole golf course.

Paris Landing, another of
Tennessee's state parks, has
a full service marina, a
magnificent bridge and a
campsite.

The Mississippi River is
plied by many old-
fashioned stern-wheelers,
all painted-up and
prettified.

The Great Smoky Mountains are a mysterious place; an ancient and brooding link in the 250-million-year-old Appalachian chain.

The statue of Authority keeps a watchful eye open outside the Shelby County Courthouse near Memphis.

The name of Elvis Presley is closely linked with Tennessee, the King having made its capital, Memphis, his home.

Early morning mist blurs the line of symmetry where water meets land at this lake in the Smoky Mountains.

One man and his dog, Spring Hill, Tennessee.

*The tradition of writing
and performing country
music is as strong in
Tennessee today as it ever
was.*

*The River Walk in Memphis
reproduces to scale the
course of the Mississippi
between Cairo and New
Orleans.*

*Memphis, Tennessee, on the
banks of the Mississippi: it's
the stuff country music
songs are written about.*

The shows at Opryland's Theater by the Lake feature chorus lines of talented and enthusiastic young artists.

Opryland in Nashville maintains the tradition of good old American Country Music, wrapped in gingham and frills.

Below: glowing with all the benefits that youth and education endow, these students at the University of the South at Sewanee look to have the confidence to take on the world.

The town of Rugby in the Cumberlands was founded in 1880 by the English social reformer Thomas Hughes. It provides an enjoyable and educational day's entertainment (facing page) for all the family.

Large or small, the glorious paddle-steamers that grace the Mississippi evoke a unique sense of the Old South.

Pigeon Forge, just south of Knoxville, is alight with neon long after dark has shrouded the Great Smoky Mountains.

Stones River National Cemetery is the resting place for the Union dead of the bloody Civil War battle fought there in 1862.

Vine Hill near Columbia is a fine example of the mansions that are associated with the tradition of Old South architecture.

This little Mennonite girl appears very pensive as she hides behind her family's barn in Tennessee.

Below: Lookout Mountain in Chattanooga National Military Park, with views across the Tennessee River.

Right: the reconstructed home of Davy Crockett in Rutherford, a unique insight into the life of a frontiersman.

Above: how true it is that those with the gift of music will never be short of friends, and, in this case, followers.

The fun at Opryland doesn't stop at musical entertainment; there are water rides and an adventure park too.

NORTH

CAROLINA

The incomparable glory of a Great Smoky Mountain sunset.

The causeway over Roanoke Sound links Roanoke and Bodie islands.

Blue-white against the greens of nature, the Baptist Church in Bethel is a positive inspiration to its congregation.

Above: south of Asheville, the view from the Blue Ridge Parkway often includes low-lying cloud in the valleys.

Below: Cape Hatteras Lighthouse is painted in a distinctive spiral pattern and warns ships off the Diamond Shoals.

"In country places plain old men have rosy faces."

Above: Brinegar Cabin at Doughton Park, once the humble home of a country weaver, now a rustic craft shop.

Where Looking Glass Creek cascades over the smooth face of Sliding Rock a natural waterslide is created.

Below: the suspended footbridge near Salva provides an alternative to wet feet, but it's not for the faint-hearted.

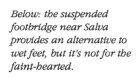

These boys are off fishing at Ocracoke Island where the waters of Pamlico Sound and the Pacific Ocean lap the shore.

From a hanglider there's a magnificent view of the Blue Ridge Mountains around Grandfather Mountain.

Nags Head Pier is obviously the place to hang out for the fashionable under-fifteens.

The quiet, sheltered waters off Nags Head are an ideal place for the uninitiated to launch their catamaran.

At Skyland, near Asheville, ballooning may be enjoyed by the active enthusiast and the land-lubbing spectator alike.

A morning coffee in a café at Nags Head, with a copy of the day's paper, is a civilized way to start the day.

The dome of the Henderson County Courthouse in Hendersonville is topped by the figure of Justice with her scales.

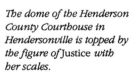

Riding off into the sunset. The locals have established many ways of conquering the state's mountainous terrain.

Below: the Great Smoky Mountains National Park offers acre upon acre of woodland, valley and mountain.

There's no shortage of rooms off the highways that wander through North Carolina's mountain scenery.

SOUTH

CAROLINA

*The Blue Ridge Mountains
wend their scenic way
through South Carolina.*

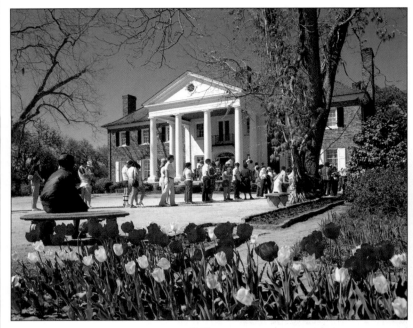

Another way to explore Cypress Gardens is by boat, maneuvering between the buttress roots in the river.

Boone Hall Plantation near Charleston is a 1935 reconstruction of the original house, which fell into ruin.

The azalea-lined trails through Cypress Gardens are hard baked from the South Carolina sun.

The Palmetto Light Artillery Re-enactment Society, at the Union County Bicentennial, Rose Hill State Park.

Above: Ceasar's Head State Park, from where some of the State's most beautiful scenery may be viewed.

The Lady Hilda *and friends moored at Fripp Island, off the Atlantic coast in Beaufort County, South Carolina.*

Down on the sands at
Myrtle Beach the dawn
attracts fishermen with a
passion for their sport.

Below: the State House in
Columbia; the capital city
of South Carolina was
established in the late
1780s.

The Adventure is a replica
of a seventeenth-century
trading ketch at historic
Charles Towne Landing.

An intra-coastal waterway near Murrells Inlet provides a peaceful spot for boating and fishing.

The houses on Rutledge Avenue overlooking Colonial Lake in Charleston are elegant and refined.

Right: Falls Cottage, near the Reedy River Falls Historic Park where the town of Greenville was founded in 1797.

Facing page top: the area around Charleston is full of history and rural scenery and is an excellent place for a family trip.

Facing page bottom: the Spartanburg High School Quintet, preparing for a performance at Rose Hill mansion.

Brood mares grazing lazily in the last hours of daylight near Greenville.

"What do you say we go Club Class next trip? Economy is beginning to get me down."

Pier 14 on Myrtle Beach, part of the fifty-five-mile-long string of beaches known as the "Grand Strand."

The Hampton Plantation at McClellanville once received George Washington himself.

Lowndes House in South Carolina is a fine example of the classic antebellum plantation house.

Hilton Head Island, settled by the English in the early 1770s, boasts many miles of unspoilt beach.

GEORGIA

Georgia's Jekyll Island is famous for its luxury cottages, of which Rockefeller's is surely one of the finest.

One of the Jekyll Island "cottages" for which the small island reached by a causeway from Brunswick is famous.

The Federal Building and United States Court House in Macon, one of the town's many handsome buildings.

Atlanta is at once a very modern city and an historic one. The downtown area comes into the former category.

The city of Savannah was established in 1733 by J. E. Oglethorpe and was Georgia's capital until 1782.

All that's old and beautiful is treasured in Savannah, from vintage cars to entire streets of elegant houses.

Savannah River at night, twinkling with lights and spanned by a skeletal bridge.

Green Meldrim House in Savannah, birthplace of Juliette Gordon Low, the founder of the Girl Scouts of America.

The handsome City Hall in Athens is one of that town's many classically influenced buildings.

Facing page: Georgia's state capitol in Atlanta is a magnificent golden-domed building of high architectural merit.

The pretty 1855 Lapham-Patterson House is found in Thomasville, the highest town in southwest Georgia.

Pebble Hill Plantation near Thomasville was designed by Abraham Garfield and features an elegant loggia.

Westville Village in Lumpkin, a fifty-seven-acre living-history village where the visitor can travel back into the 1850s.

Approximately the same size as Florida but with only half its population, Georgia's rural areas are vast.

Stone Mountain Park contains the biggest exposed granite mass in the world, upon which is a huge relief sculpture.

There's lots of space for long drives down the fairway in the wide open spaces of Georgia's many golf clubs.

Frills and flowers and a friendly face.

"Easy Riders," near Dillard.

Earnest gesticulation between father and son on the Sea Islands, originally settled by escaped Creole slaves.

The dugouts at Fort McAllister formed the southernmost fortification of Savannah's coast during the Civil War.

It is on the site of Christ Church in Frederica that John and Charles Wesley were thought to have preached in 1776.

This girl from the Sea Islands might grow up speaking "Gullah," a dialect unique to the Islands' black residents.

FLORIDA

The silhouettes and shadows of a sunset in Cypress Gardens are a magical sight.

The nineteenth-century nine-room frame house of the Kingsley Plantation on Fort George Island is open to the public.

Shuffleboard is good excercise for Florida's Golden Girls who seem to find long life and happiness in the state.

Miami's Indian name, Mayaimi, is thought to mean either "big" or "sweet water," either of which would still apply.

Fishing straight off the beach is a luxury few places offer, but the warm waters that lap Miami are special.

Gaily-colored sails atop fleet catamarans make a pleasing sight on the palm-lined, sandy beach at West Key.

Below: melting slowly into the ocean, the sun puts in a long day's work in Florida almost every day of the year.

The Everglades is a unique wilderness area in southern Florida that shelters many rare species of flora and fauna.

Circus World in Orlando boasts that it provides a whole day's family entertainment, with a fairground, shows ... and clowns.

Saint Petersburg (below), with its peaceful marina, has become the fashionable place to go for sunshine vacations on Florida's West Coast.

Living proof that the appeal of Disney World spans the generations – in fact it is the child that appears least inspired!

"As the parade passes by..." the audience at Disney World show their appreciation with cheers and applause.

The spirit of the riverboat era captures the feeling of escapism inherent in the Disney World philosophy.

Donald, Mickey, Goofy, Pluto and Minnie with new-found friends at Disney World, Orlando, Florida.

Noses and knees, intent on the parade at Disney World.

119

The World's Greatest Great Grandpa ... and the world's most talented great grandson? The beat goes on in Florida.

Saint Petersburg, on Florida's west coast, is best-known as a retirement center – a good place for restaurateurs.

It's not all clear skies in the
Sunshine State: into each
life some rain must fall.

Below: putting on the style
at Palm Beach; this smartly
dressed lady seems to be
using her umbrella as a
parasol.

The Great White Heron lives in large numbers in the wildlife refuge created especially for it near Key West.

An unusual competition is held off the coast of Florida once a year – a man-powered-submarine race.

The islands of the Evergaldes provide perhaps the last bastion for many unique species of flora and fauna.

The sunny beaches of Fort Lauderdale provide an idyllic spot for a few hours of après retirement relaxation.

ALABAMA

The Japanese Gardens in Birmingham.

The Confederate Monument in Montgomery, a towering witness to the Confederate dead of the Civil War.

Martin Luther King Jr. became minister of a baptist church in Montgomery in 1954 and is memorialized there today.

As well as having more miles of navigable river than any other state, Alabama also has seas full of fish.

The agricultural area around Courtland, up in the far north of the state, is blessed with both fertility and beauty.

Mobile is an historic town with a cosmopolitan background, having been occupied by the French, British and Spanish.

Alabama benefits from having more than twenty state parks and over ten national forest recreation areas.

Natural beauty abounds in the Heart of Dixie; a solitary heron perfects the scene by the sea near Fort Morgan.

DeSoto Falls State Park near Fort Payne offers camping, boating, fishing, accommodation and eating facilities.

At Noccalula Falls Park in Gadsden a reconstructed pioneer village may be found with many interesting exhibits.

"Remember that the most beautiful things in the world are the most useless; peacocks and lilies for instance." Ruskin.

Alabama's State Capitol in Montgomery, where Jefferson Davis was sworn in as president of the Confederacy in 1861.

The Shorter Mansion in Eufaula is now a museum of State history and Confederate memorabilia.

The First White House of the Confederacy was occupied by Jefferson Davis for just three months of his presidency.

A Southern Belle,
Bellingham Gardens,
Alabama.

MISSISSIPPI

De Soto Lake in Coahoma County.

Depicting scenes from the Civil War, sculptures of great passion are found at the battlefield at Vicksburg.

Dusk colors the sky over Moon Lake north of Friars Point in Coahoma County, silhouetting the tumbledown pier.

Grand Gulf was once a town of major import in Mississippi, rivaling Natchez, but today it serves mainly as an historic park.

If you look closely you can discover a family of turtles making their way along a fallen tree.

There's nothing more tranquil than fishing in Perry Martin Lake in the Great River Road State Park at Rosedale.

Cotton, that versatile and lucrative product, grows in great quantities over vast areas of Mississippi.

Biloxi is a coastal resort full of historic buildings that bear witness to the area's Spanish and French occupation.

The Mississippi River near Mayersville, where yellow sunflowers complement the blue of the water and sky.

Melrose is a fine house built between 1841 and 1845 on a large, English-country-house-style estate in Natchez.

Vicksburg National Military Park is the site of numerous monuments, sculptures, statues, memorials and exhibits.

The town of Vicksburg was settled as long ago as 1790 by the Spanish – who called it walnut trees: "Nogales."

Ducks Not Welcome.

Elegant porches are perhaps what the Southern home is best known for; on Commerce St., Natchez, the tradition continues.

The Illinois Memorial, the interior of which bears the names of that state's soldiers who fought in the Vicksburg campaigns.

LOUISIANA

New Orleans: the soul of the South.

700, Royal Street in New Orleans, with its fine iron-work balconies, was built by Jean LaBrance in 1835.

" ... then the other guy said 'I bet I can eat ten'!"

Ladies of the Deep South keeping up the tradition of quilting, and, no doubt, the even older one of gossiping.

Oak Alley Plantation, near New Orleans, is famous for its avenue of live oak trees which stretches a full quarter mile.

An image many will associate with Southern Louisiana: the grace and luxury of life on a plantation.

Buttress roots, another distinct image of the South, which boasts much in the way of unusual flora and fauna.

*Bowed and bonnetted,
these ladies in Morgan City
seem to be enjoying
themselves enormously.*

*Dancing and having a
high old time in the open
air is synonymous with the
spirit of the South in
Louisiana.*

The Myrtles in St. Francisville is a carefully restored plantation house with a hundred-and-ten-foot gallery.

Rosedown Plantation, surely one of the finest homes in the state, was built for Martha Hilliard Barrow and Daniel Turnbull.

A New Orleans street trader leads a blessed existence when the weather is fine and the tourists are spending freely.

The Rural Life Museum recreates the living conditions of days gone by in rural Louisiana.

New Orleans' Mardi Gras festival provides ample opportunity for everybody to bring out their favorite hats.

Floats included in the Mardi Gras procession have often been worked on for the whole of the preceeding year.

Clowns with rainbow hair and pompom buttons are all part of the scene on the streets of festive New Orleans.

Entire families of clowns parade in the Vieux Carré on "Fat Tuesday," complete with family car and balloons.

Imagination, inspiration, collaboration and perspiration are all essential ingredients of the build-up to Mardi Gras.

153

*Gritted teeth and flapping
flanges at a Southern
Louisiana Rodeo Show
where the dust isn't the
only thing that flies.*

Ardoyne, near Houma, was built in 1900 as a copy of a castle in Scotland and has twenty-one rooms.

Whoa! Hold him tight, don't let him get away!

Saint Charles Avenue in New Orleans is the site of the many opulent town homes of Louisiana's plantation families.

Mules, donkeys and horses all find employment in the Vieux Carré, pulling various cargoes of keen sightseers.

Jazz was born in New Orleans and still makes its home there, providing the finest sounds in the South.

"Sleepy time down South."

Below: music resonates throughout the city of New Orleans from the clubs to the streets and doorways.

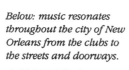

The harvest of the sea is bounteous off Louisiana's shores, where this mother and her child have caught some shrimp.

"Ol' Man River" just keeps rolling along beside New Orleans, plied by paddle-wheelers and oil tankers alike.

Even Southern Belles grow old. "A lady of a 'certain age,' which means Certainly aged." Byron.

The Natchez *steamboat paddles away on a cruise up the Mississippi River in New Orleans, Louisiana.*